BRITISH ART MEDALS
1982 - 2002

Sponsored by **DNW**
DIX · NOONAN · WEBB
AUCTIONEERS AND VALUERS

Published by the British Art Medal Trust, London, 2002

ISBN 0 9536988 3 1

Design by Bubble Design
Bubble_design@lycos.co.uk

Typeset by Galata Print
The Old White Lion,
Llanfyllin, Powys SY22 5BX

Printed by Pardy & Son
Parkside, Ringwood, Hampshire

Philip Attwood is editor of *The Medal*,
a secretary of the British Art Medal Society,
and a curator in the British Museum's
Department of Coins and Medals

Front and back covers: *Past and Present* by Rob Wood (156)
This page: *Sheep Moor II* by Ron Dutton (4)
Page 4: *Charles Dickens* by Ronald Searle (27)

BRITISH ART MEDALS
1982 - 2002

CONTENTS

INTRODUCTION

This book has two principal aims. One is to celebrate twenty years of the British Art Medal Society (BAMS), and to look back at the medals issued by the society over that period and at the other activities organised by the society. The other is to introduce the subject to those unaware of the versatility of the medal, and in particular the contemporary medal, through a presentation of those issued by the society. Artists, collectors, art college lecturers and their students, and many others have felt the fascination that the medium can exert, thanks to the efforts of BAMS.

The first two sections of this book serve as brief introductions to the art medal in general and to BAMS in particular. The third section looks at the artists who have made medals for the society, and asks where the appeal lies for contemporary artists. The fourth considers the wide range of medals that the society has issued over the last twenty years, and examines the attraction felt by collectors. The fifth section is concerned with the society's Student Medal Project, initiated in 1993 in order to increase the attention given to the medium of the medal in art colleges, and indicates just some of the ways that college lecturers have found the medal can help their courses. The sixth and final section looks at the subject from the point of view of the individual or organisation who wishes to commission a medal, and gives some guidance on how to take this most rewarding of steps.

The book includes a complete list of the medals issued by BAMS during its first twenty years. It is regretted that considerations of space have precluded the illustration here of all the medals . However, all are reproduced in the various issues of *The Medal* and on the society's website (www.bams.org.uk/).

Acknowledgments

David Attwood, Peter Bagwell Purefoy, Geoffrey Clarke, RA, Lord Cunliffe, Stephen Dodd, Ron Dutton, Konrad Elsdon, Antony Griffiths, Irene Gunston, Mark Jones, Janet Larkin, Marcy Leavitt Bourne, Jeremy Lever, QC, Jane McAdam Freud, Roger McGough, OBE, Dhruva Mistry, CBE, RA, Jennifer Montagu, FBA, Nicola Moss, Tom Phillips, RA, Professor Lord Renfrew of Kaimsthorn, FBA, Michael Sandle, Donald Scarinci, Howard and Frances Simmons, Danuta Solowiej, Rachel Ward, Marina Warner, Bill Woodrow.

All the medals reproduced here were issued by the British Art Medal Society, excepting those on pp. 6, 7, 44-7.

1 What is a medal?

To most people the word 'medal' brings to mind the
awards given for acts of valour or the prizes
for which athletes and other sportsmen and women
compete. But, in reality, these two different types
of medal represent offshoots of a much older and
more intriguing tradition.

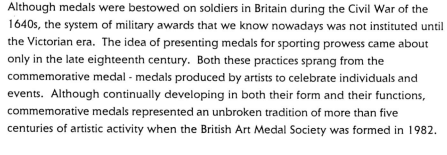

Although medals were bestowed on soldiers in Britain during the Civil War of the 1640s, the system of military awards that we know nowadays was not instituted until the Victorian era. The idea of presenting medals for sporting prowess came about only in the late eighteenth century. Both these practices sprang from the commemorative medal - medals produced by artists to celebrate individuals and events. Although continually developing in both their form and their functions, commemorative medals represented an unbroken tradition of more than five centuries of artistic activity when the British Art Medal Society was formed in 1982.

The earliest medals were made in Renaissance Italy in the first half of the fifteenth century. Thinking to emulate figures from the ancient world, princes and other cultured individuals had themselves portrayed on one side of their medals, whilst the other side was generally reserved for a personal device symbolising the particular virtues with which that individual wished to be associated. The celebrated painter Antonio Pisano (known as Pisanello) designed and modelled some of the earliest examples, and other famous artists - painters, sculptors, and others - were quick to follow. These medals generally served as gifts, and were presented to princes, friends, and followers. Made of metal, they were also intended to preserve the memory of the individual for posterity, just as the ancient coins that were being dug up all over Italy were perceived as witnesses to the likenesses and deeds of Roman figures of the classical period.

In the early sixteenth century the fashion for medals spread to Germany and the Netherlands, and the nature of the medal began to alter in a number of significant ways. Whereas the earliest medals had generally been cast in relatively small editions, the sixteenth century saw an increasing use in the technique of striking, a method of manufacture that made it easier to make large numbers of one particular design. The sorts of messages conveyed by the medals' reverses also underwent a change in emphasis at this time, with events rather than human qualities being increasingly celebrated, and overt political messages taking the place of the earlier, often enigmatic, emblems. The sixteenth-century goldsmith Benvenuto Cellini was amongst those artists who turned his hand to medals, making some that, his contemporary Giorgio Vasari wrote, 'were executed with incredible care, and cannot be praised enough'.

Pisanello's cast bronze medal of Leonello d'Este, lord of Ferrara, of around 1441 (left) has as its reverse an allegory, the precise significance of which is now unknown. Cellini's medal of Pope Clement VII of 1534 (above) is more readily understandable: it celebrates the peace then reigning in Italy; the medal is struck in silver. Around 1900 French artists began to produce works that departed from the circular form and the commemorative function, such as Alphonse Lechevrel's **History records the discoveries of archaeology** *(below). This medal was issued in 1904 by the Société des Amis de la Médaille Française, a Paris-based society that was in many ways a fore-runner of the British Art Medal Society.*

A further proliferation in medallic types occurred during the succeeding centuries, as the medium was taken up in countries throughout Europe, and the purposes to which medals were put expanded. In the nineteenth century the mechanisation of medal production resulted in large numbers of struck medals being made in countries around the world, including many of high artistic merit. Towards the end of the nineteenth century a new development saw the medal develop into an art form independent of commemoration and other practical functions, when various French artists began to make medals that were self-contained works of art in the manner of sculptures and paintings.

The twentieth century witnessed a continuing use of the art medal as a vehicle for personal expression on the part of artists. This resulted in contemplative works of great beauty and also in medals that made incisive comments on the world in which they were produced. During the First World War, German medallists used an Expressionist style to comment on the horror of the conflict and to make propaganda points. In the 1920s and 1930s, French artists produced medals in a sharp-edged Art Deco style, which combined allusions to the ancient world with a distinctive brand of modernism. In the decades following the Second World War, artists in several eastern European countries - in particular, Poland, Czechoslovakia, and Hungary - expanded the boundaries further, using techniques and materials that were new to the medal, making glass medals, medals into which ready-made objects were incorporated, and abstract medals. Subsequently, countries such as the Netherlands and Portugal also became centres of exciting experimental work.

The variety of forms taken by the modern medal has sometimes led to doubts being expressed as to whether the term still has any meaning. But, although many of the traditional attributes of the medal - made of metal, circular, two-sided, combining images and text, and of a size that can be held comfortably in the hand - are often dispensed with, most contemporary medals possess at least some of these characteristics. Modern medals are perhaps best defined in that they are produced by artists who see themselves working within the tradition outlined above (although often pushing at its limits). But, on the whole, it may be best not to attempt a rigid definition. This is by no means the only area of contemporary art in which boundaries have become blurred, and it is enough that the objects, however they are termed, engage and stimulate the viewer and holder.

76

119

Contemporary medals can take many forms. Rob Kesseler's **Book of Leaves** (76), issued by BAMS in 1991, is 'an object of contemplation, a touchstone for the memory of things seen and read'.

Blessed are the Peacemakers for they shall be called the Sons of God, by Anne-Marie Watkins (119), is one of a series of works based on the Beatitudes of the Bible that was issued by the society in 1996. Fitting into the hand like a grenade, the medal's form evokes Christ's injunction, 'Let your light so shine before men, that they may see your good works'; above, a tiny soldier peers into the unknown. Also far removed from the traditional medal is Alison Branagan's **Gamut in an Armoire** (145-6), which substitutes exterior/interior for the more traditional obverse/reverse. Rather than commemorating a specific event, this medal is concerned with memory itself, and the emotions that we all carry.

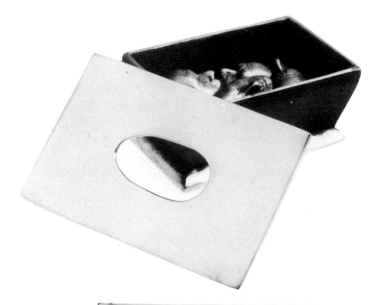

145-6

50

Some of the artists commissioned by BAMS have produced medals that relate directly to the society and its activities. The medal by Slovak artist Marián Polonsky, commissioned in 1989 but not completed until 1992, is entitled *A Medal for BAMS* (89): its subject is itself. The Lake District, the setting for the society's 1987 weekend conference, served as the inspiration for *Diary* by José Aurelio (50); the Portuguese sculptor was invited to take part in the weekend as a guest lecturer.

89

2 What is BAMS?

*The British Art Medal Society was founded in 1982,
at a time when medal making in Britain was just
beginning to revive. Its aim was, and remains,
'to encourage, develop and support the practice
and study of medallic art'.*

Medals had long been made in this country. Italian and Netherlandish medallists worked in Britain in the sixteenth century, and the miniaturist Nicholas Hilliard produced exquisite gold medals of Elizabeth I and James I. Over the centuries that followed struck medals were produced by the engravers attached to the Royal Mint, the most celebrated being the nineteenth-century artist William Wyon, who in 1838 was elected as a Royal Academician because of his work in the medium. In the 1880s the cast medal was revived through the efforts of the painter Alphonse Legros, who formed a Society of Medallists, the aim of which was to promote a return to the principles of Italian Renaissance medals; the society had close connections with the contemporaneous arts and crafts movement, with which it had shared ideals relating to artistic merit. It did not, however, survive the First World War, and, although a few artists, such as the sculptor Gilbert Bayes, produced interesting work in the first half of the twentieth century, the medium went into decline.

In the years following the Second World War very few medals of any quality were produced in Britain, but in the 1970s this situation began to change, as British artists again turned to the medal. This increased level of activity was reflected in the larger British contribution to the biennial exhibitions of contemporary medals from around the world organised by the Fédération Internationale de la Médaille (FIDEM). London's Worshipful Company of Goldsmiths encouraged interest by holding a number of exhibitions featuring British medallic work by artists as diverse as the painter John Piper, the sculptor Geoffrey Clarke, and the engraver Malcolm Appleby.

1

In 1979 the Royal Society of Arts awarded a scholarship to the sculptor Ron Dutton, who then taught in the fine art department of Wolverhampton Polytechnic (now University), to enable him to travel to Finland, to make a study of the Finnish Medal Guild, which had been established in 1965. Dutton's subsequent report proposed that a British society should be formed, which would commission medals from contemporary artists and offer them for sale to its members. A preliminary meeting of interested people was held at the Royal Society of Arts in February 1982, and the society's inaugural meeting, attended by twenty-eight, was held in the same venue on 27 April. Graham Pollard, deputy director and curator of medals of the Fitzwilliam Museum, Cambridge, was elected as chairman, and the new society's other offices were taken by Ron Dutton, Terence Mullaly, art critic of the *Daily Telegraph*, and Mark Jones, curator of medals at the British Museum.

Among the first medals to be issued by BAMS in 1982 were Jane McAdam Freud's **Picasso** (1) and Nigel Hall's **Bronze Shoal** (5). Hall's medal suggests the movement of shoals of fish, its unusual form evoking the transparency of water.

The society went into action immediately, and its membership began to rise. The first issue of its journal, *The Medal*, appeared in the summer of 1982, and offered to the membership medals by Ron Dutton, Jane McAdam Freud, Mark Holloway, Jacqueline Stieger, and Nigel Hall. The society's first exhibition, of Hungarian medals, was put on in 1984, travelling to Wolverhampton Art Gallery, Goldsmiths' Hall, London, Christ Church Oxford, and Gateshead's Shipley Art Gallery. In the same year the British Art Medal Trust was set up to handle charitable activities, notably the journal and other publications and educational activities. The first weekend conference was held in May 1985, in a splendid Lutyens country-house outside Southampton, which had just been converted into a conference centre. A visit to the Royal Mint took place in October 1985, and the society's first series of winter lectures was held at London's Warburg Institute a few months later.

These have since remained the principal activities of the society, under the presidency of Terence Mullaly, who succeeded Graham Pollard in 1986, and latterly of Mark Jones. Membership soon became international, and now there are members in thirty-four countries around the world. In the first twenty years 161 medals by 122 different artists have been issued (these are listed on pp. 51-5); the majority of these have been cast, but there have also been several struck pieces. In all, over five thousand individual works have been produced, most of which have been purchased by members (the artist retains two examples of his or her medal, and two more go to the society's own collection). Forty issues of *The Medal* have appeared, and the journal has established itself as the world leader in its subject; published biannually, in March and September, it contains articles relating to both historical and contemporary medals, book reviews, news items from around the world, and information on the society's new medal issues. The weekend conferences have continued to be held in a different venue each year. These have included Durham, Cirencester, St Ives, Portmeirion, Glasgow, Kendal, Edinburgh, Cambridge, and also two venues abroad: Chatelperron in the Bourbonnais region of France and Cork in the Republic of Ireland. Talks by artists and academics, visits to places of interest, and practical workshops at which members try their hand at various medal-making skills are standard elements of these weekends. The winter lectures, now held in the elegant surroundings of the Worshipful Company of Cutlers, are also given by a mix of artists and specialists, and cover both contemporary and historical subjects. Visits continue to be organised, to exhibitions, foundries, and other places of interest, and the society also has its own exhibition programme.

The society also coordinates the British contribution to the biennial international exhibitions of contemporary medals staged by FIDEM. In 1992 this exhibition was held in London, at the British Museum; the conference held to coincide with it was hosted by BAMS, and was also centred in the museum. Just as the nineteenth-century Society of Medallists was actively supported by members of the Department of Coins and Medals of the British Museum, so BAMS continues to enjoy the support and encouragement of the museum in the twenty-first century. The address of the society has from the beginning been c/o Department of Coins and Medals, British Museum, and the museum and society work closely together to promote a wider interest in the medal.

Recognising the diverse nature of its members and their particular interests, the society has various categories of membership. Ordinary members buy at least one medal from the society each year. Associate members pay a little more, but are not obliged to buy any medals (although they can do so if they wish). The society also offers corporate membership, and there is a reduced membership rate for full-time students, many of whom discover the medal while at art college. All members receive *The Medal*, and are welcome at all the society's events, where, as one sculptor has described it, stimulation is provided by 'meeting all sorts of people with very different perspectives'. Among these people are collectors and dealers, artists and academics, all of whom find that they have much to learn from one another.

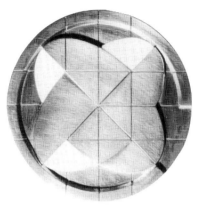 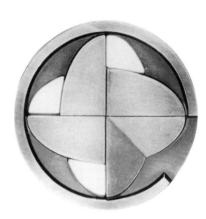

8

*BAMS has issued both struck and cast medals. John Maine's **Turning Circle** (8, 25) was struck in silver and bronze versions, and Felicity Powell's poetic image of time passing was struck in silver in the year 2000 as a millennium issue (147). Most of the society's medals have, however, been cast in bronze. These include Jacqueline Stieger's **Food Furrows** (3), Dhruva Mistry's **Maya Medallion** (52) and Irene Gunston's **Undisturbed Night** (137).*

 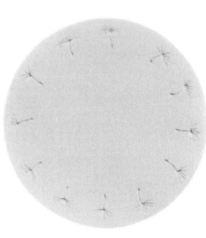

147

3

52

137

3 The medallists: artists who make medals

No artists restrict themselves entirely to medals.
The first artist to work in the medium, the
fifteenth-century Pisanello, was a painter, and
signed his medals as such: OPVS PISANI PICTORIS
(The work of Pisano, the painter).

Later artists who made medals were often sculptors or goldsmiths, or engravers of coin dies, but they were also drawn from other specialities. Today the range is equally broad, as is made clear by the diversity of the artists who have produced medals for BAMS.

Many contemporary British sculptors have found that the small scale of the medal offers possibilities that complement their larger works, and that the tension that exists between the medal's two sides provides a format that helps them further develop their ideas. Bill Woodrow comments on his experience of producing *Our World* for BAMS in 1997: 'I particularly enjoyed working within the restrictions (self-imposed) of my notion of a classical medal, ie. small scale, two sides, and an edge that held text. The idea that I was making a medal (in this case to celebrate a relationship and its component parts) and not a small sculpture was crucial to my thinking and the resultant form.'

As an object that is held in the hand, the medal has an intimacy that allows the sculptor to communicate on a more immediately personal level than is possible from an open site in a sculpture park or a plinth in a city square. Moreover, small in scale does not mean small in scope. Geoffrey Clarke, RA, refers to the medal as 'a kind of Gulliver experience': 'Treasure the minute', he advises, 'keep searching the tiny image and traverse the landscape of the palm. Reinterpret the vast concepts in the mind... Contemplate, search and discover.' Those sculptors besides Woodrow and Clarke who have made medals for the society include Lynn Chadwick, Ian Hamilton Finlay, Jonah Jones, John Maine, RA, Nigel Hall, Dhruva Mistry, RA, and Michael Sandle. Sandle's BAMS piece, *Belgrano Medal - a Medal of Dishonour*, was the artist's first medal, and he readily admits that it was surprisingly difficult to do. Dhruva Mistry also points out that, 'Making a good medal is a highly challenging task for an artist'. But, paradoxically, the very restrictions that the medium imposes can also be liberating influences.

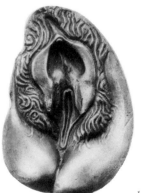

128

18

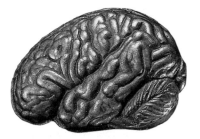

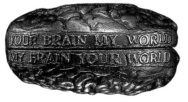

128

*Among the internationally renowned sculptors who have produced medals for BAMS is Lynn Chadwick, whose **Diamond** (18), issued in 1984, has since become highly collectible. The two-part medal by Bill Woodrow, entitled **Our World** (128), celebrates the relationship between the sexes and the interrelation between the mind and sexuality.*

More used to working on a small scale are the jewellers and silversmiths who have received commissions from BAMS, and who have applied to the medal their own techniques, including engraving and enamelling. Among them are such well-known practitioners as Fred Rich, Malcolm Appleby, and Kevin Coates. Other BAMS artists have come from other widely differing backgrounds. The celebrated Liverpool poet Roger McGough created a medal for the society in 1998. Ronald Pennell, one of the country's foremost glass-engravers, has made two medals for the society. The cartoonist and creator of the St Trinian's girls, Ronald Searle, whose first medals were issued by the French mint in the 1970s, has made no less than seven medals for BAMS. And Tom Phillips, RA, who first made his name in the 1960s as a painter, and has since developed an extraordinarily wide range of activities, produced a medal for BAMS in 1994. Making a medal was a rewarding experience for Phillips, who writes: 'Tondos and roundels have always intrigued me as a painter and I relished the chance to explore the circular format in relief. Every artist is enriched by new forms, materials and techniques: even in this so far single essay I learned a lot.' Roger McGough also welcomed this extension of his activities, commenting: 'To be honest, I am surprised there aren't more collaborations between poets and medal-makers. The poet is a miniaturist, and I greatly enjoyed the experience of choosing a short poem and seeing it transformed into something magically tangible.'

As well as commissioning medals from figures who enjoy international prestige in the wider art world, BAMS has issued works by artists who have come to value especially the possibilities afforded by the medium, and have made it something of a speciality within their oeuvre. Medals have also been commissioned from art students and recent graduates who have shown exceptional ability. Although most of the artists whose medals have been issued by the society work in Britain, BAMS has also recognised the importance of bringing artists from other countries to the notice of British collectors. Accordingly, medals have been commissioned from

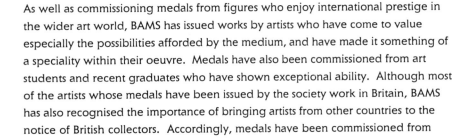

artists from several other European countries, including the Netherlands, Italy, Portugal, Germany, Sweden, Poland, Hungary, Bulgaria, and Ukraine, and also from others working further afield, in the United States, Canada, and Australia.

The activities of the society have helped many artists from many different backgrounds to realise the opportunities offered by the medal. For Geoffrey Clarke the appeal lies in part in the possibility of 'instant expression, a permanence and a quality in the palm of the hand ... plasticine, a naked light, searching spontaneous marks, half-closed eyes and the magic begins'. The medallic form gives artists a framework within which to explore both ideas and techniques: experimenting with the form, with the two sides, with the edge; merging the visual with the tactile; playing with positive and negative; combining images and words; modelling in wax or clay; carving in wood or stone; engraving into crystal or hard metals; patinating and burnishing - the possibilities are endless.

*These two medals are by sculptors who are also Royal Academicians. Geoffrey Clarke's **Nature and Time** (143) was produced for the new millennium, and places humanity in the context of the natural landscape and the passage of the years, whilst Dhruva Mistry's **Humanity Medal** (125) offers hope of peace to a troubled planet.*

143

125

10

80

131

The great variety of BAMS medals reflects the different backgrounds of the artists. The jeweller Fred Rich used enamels and a tassel to provide extra colour in his **Osprey** medal (10). The force of Malcolm Appleby's **Parma** medal (80-81) derives in large part from the artist's skill as an engraver. **In Good Hands**, modelled after a design by Roger McGough (131), incorporates a succinct and witty verse by the poet. **The Vellinger Medal** (106), an enigmatic piece inspired by a 1943 novel, *Unhaunted comma*, is by Tom Phillips, one of Britain's leading painters.

106

67

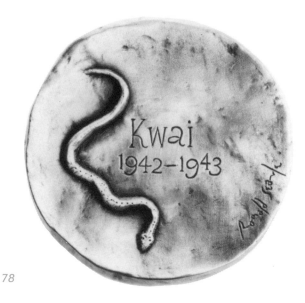

78

Among the medals created for BAMS by
cartoonist Ronald Searle is the humorous
Searle at Seventy (67), produced for his
seventieth birthday - 'Already?', asks the
artist, who is shown as the legendary
Laocoön grappling with the snake.
In contrast, the sombre **Kwai 50th
Anniversary Medal** (78) harks back to
Searle's experience as a prisoner-of-war
working on the Thai-Burma railway.

85

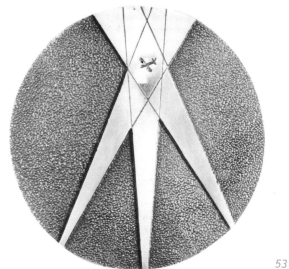

53

BAMS has commissioned medals from artists from many countries. Internationalism is a feature of the German Werner Niermann's **Epidaurus** (85), which was inspired by regular visits to Greece, and also of the Australian Michael Meszaros's **Battle of Britain** (53). In his **The Garden of Eden** (132), Netherlandish artist Gustaaf Hellegers contrasts human aspirations with the fear of the unknown.

132

135

The formerly communist countries of eastern Europe have produced many fine medallists. Among the medals issued by the British Art Medal Society have been **The Dreamer** by Polish artist Stanislaw Cukier (135) and **Head** by the Hungarian János Kalmár (21). From Bulgaria, Ivanka Mincheva's **The Cruel Ocean** (57) bears a couplet from a ballad by John Gay, and **Acta est Fabula** by Bogomil Nikolov (62) comments on the inherent instability of all social and political structures - the play is never finished!

21

57

62

4 An infinite variety: collecting art medals

Produced in editions (the edition of each BAMS medal is limited to one hundred), medals are similar to prints in that each one is an original work. Their relatively small size and low cost make them readily affordable.

The different techniques employed to make them, the range of metals used, and the different processes that can be applied to finish them, all contribute to the variety found in modern medals. But more important is what the artists bring in terms of individual thought and expression: each medal is a very personal statement, offering insights and perspectives in which the collector is invited to share.

Tactile as much as visual objects, medals are experienced by being held and turned. Illustrations in a book can convey fully neither the quality of physicality they possess nor the pleasure to be gained from observing first one side and then the other, from turning the piece over again, holding it in the palm of the hand, feeling the rounded surfaces, the cold metal. Although some collectors like to keep their medals in cabinets, many have at least some readily accessible, so that they can be picked up and enjoyed at will. Desks, bookshelves, mantelpieces, all provide suitable surfaces for these compact and compelling objects.

All collectors have their favourites. Asked to select one BAMS medal that has a particular importance for him, Mark Jones, the society's president and director of the Victoria and Albert Museum, chose Ian Hamilton Finlay's *Terror/Virtue*, issued in 1984. At the same time he admitted that it might not at first seem an obvious choice: 'Seemingly naive and formulaic, Hamilton Finlay's medal lacks sculptural or tactile quality. But of all the medals that BAMS has produced this one means most to me. In the dry visual rhyme between the guillotine and classical columns, in the brutal simplicity of the inscription, in Robespierre's accompanying quotation, "what is immoral is politically unsound, what corrupts counter-revolutionary", is a fundamental ambiguity brilliantly conveyed through the medallic medium. Are Terror and Virtue, the obverse and reverse of the medal (in 2002 as in 1792), opposed or are they inseparable? Where does the artist stand? And where do we?' The same medal has a special significance also for writer Marina Warner: 'Ian Hamilton Finlay's medal, *Terror/Virtue*, was the first medal I bought, and I still keep it by me on my desk, as a kind of warning - about lots of things. It perfectly

66

A number of artists have produced
medals honouring the passion for
collecting. In John Lobban's **Homage to
Collectors** (66) the magpie has picked up
a medal by the fifteenth-century
Pisanello and the squirrel is burying
Lynn Chadwick's BAMS medal **Diamond**
(18), whilst the reverse illustrates the joy
of the chase. Robin Ashby's **Medal
Lover** (82) represents 'the ultimate
collector, the person that simply has to
have it...'

82

15

mobilises medals' duality, their power to speak between the lines, and since September 11th its stark challenge to the classical order (of paired columns and lofty gateways and pillars of knowledge) has become even more desolate.'

Antony Griffiths, keeper of prints and drawings in the British Museum and a BAMS member, also comments on the importance of the medal's front and back: 'the greatest medals set up an interplay between the two sides that can add a remarkable resonance to the message'. Yet the medal that he singles out for special notice is a uniface piece. He explains: 'The medals that most appeal to me are those that are in the widest sense of the word "political". The medium's history is all about commemoration and the manipulation of memory. So it will be obvious why my favourite BAMS medal is Michael Sandle's *Belgrano Medal - a Medal of Dishonour*.' For centuries medals have served as vehicles for incisive comment on current events, and Sandle's medal continues this tradition. The furore provoked by the *Belgrano Medal* was greatly relished by the artist: 'What I enjoyed most was the rumpus it caused - there were questions asked in the House about it and someone was even annoyed enough to produce a counter-medal.' Medals often refuse to sit quietly on their shelves!

Medals have also traditionally been produced as acts of homage to individuals from the past or the present, with the reverse used to comment on some aspect of the person portrayed on the front. This tradition is continued in a medal of Joseph Conrad by Polish artist Ewa Olszewska-Borys, on the back of which a forceful image evokes the writer's love of the sea. This medal is a particular favourite of designer Roger Cunliffe, who explains: 'I was an avid reader of Conrad in my youth: his rich but measured prose a counterpoint to the sailor's tales he told. The medal echoes this, with the dignified portrait of Conrad on the obverse and the freely sculpted waves on the reverse. It is one of the finest examples of Ewa Olszewska-Borys's powerful yet controlled modelling.'

39

102

Political medals issued by BAMS include Ian Hamilton Finlay's **Terror/Virtue** (15) and Michael Sandle's controversial **Belgrano Medal - a Medal of Dishonour** (39), which alludes to the Falklands conflict of 1982 and shows British prime-minister Margaret Thatcher as a death's head labelled 'Shameless Empress'. Among the various tributes to celebrated individuals are **In Memory of Joseph Conrad** by Ewa Olszewska-Borys (102), whilst Carole Hodgson's **Bogman** (44) evokes instead the anonymous figures of prehistory.

44

As well as deriving inspiration from events and people, medals nowadays focus on other diverse subjects not generally associated with the medium: the natural and human-made world, myths and legends, human relationships, and other abstract concepts such as memory and dreams - indeed, more or less any aspect of life may provoke a medal. For the distinguished archaeologist Professor Lord Renfrew, director of the McDonald Institute for Archaeological Research, Cambridge, Carole Hodgson's *Bogman* stands out particularly among BAMS medals, using, as it does, 'the dark texture of bronze to resemble the leathery tissue of the bog body'. *Bogman* is a poignant work, in which, as Professor Renfrew comments, 'the millennia dissolve in an equivalency of matter'. Hodgson's medal, he writes, 'is a brilliantly evocative relic of antiquity'.

Landscape, long the preserve of painters and print-makers, has been the subject of a number of other medals issued by the society. For art historian Jennifer Montagu, 'Ron Dutton's *Sheep Moor II* was the reason I joined BAMS: I had to have it! The repeated curves - curved sheep in a curved group, curved horizon with a misty circular sun above it - play with the round shape of the medal. The varied textures are appealing and suggestive of foreground and distance, particularly as I turn it in the light (Dutton is a master of medallic light). It is a pleasing "abstract" low relief image, but there's a whole tranquil landscape held in the palm of my hand.'

The rural calm evoked by Ron Dutton contrasts sharply with the shock tactics used by Sandle. Many other ways of gaining and keeping the attention are also employed: humour, for example, as in Ronald Searle's witty self-portrait medal. The variety of contemporary medals, and of BAMS medals in particular, is widely recognised. US collector Donald Scarinci comments on the important nurturing role played by the society in 'the evolution of the British art medal from its rather ordinary pre-1980s to its extraordinary leadership in this art form today'. In Scarinci's view it is eastern Europe and the United Kingdom that now produce 'the most interesting and creative art medals in the world'. Many collectors would agree.

*Landscape plays an important role in Ron Dutton's work, as, for example, in his **Sheep Moor II** of 1982 (4).*

4

Contemporary medallists have continued the tradition of commemorating important historical events. The possibilities and problems facing the countries of eastern Europe in the aftermath of Communism are expressed, respectively, by the gateway and the menacing boulder of a medal of 1991 by Hungarian artist Enikő Szöllőssy (97). Paul Ryan marked the new millennium with **Round in Circles - Millennium Medal** (148), on which a human fingerprint is contrasted with the vastness of the solar system. The planets appear as they did on 31 December 1999.

97

148

33

37

111

73

To the propaganda medals of the past
has now been added the protest medal,
and the safeguarding of the
environment is the subject of many.
In Ronald Pennell's **A Tree for Me** (33)
the last tree is being carted off in a
wheelbarrow. Atmospheric pollution is
the subject of Malcolm Appleby's
Fall Out (37), whilst the horror of
Chernobyl is evoked by Ukrainian
medallists Oxsana Teryokhina and
Natalya Domovitskikh in a work that
incorporates a raging inferno and
Goya's famous print, *The sleep of reason
produces monsters* (111). **Save our Air
Earth Water** by Swedish sculptor Berndt
Helleberg (73) is a heart-felt plea for
clean air, earth and water, and in Linda
Crook's **Bite Back** (92) nature retaliates:
the figure, who is trying on one side of
the medal to eat too large a fish, is itself
consumed on the other side.

92

In this medal by Jacqueline Stieger (87) a town is destroyed by traffic, which also seems to cause the medal itself to crack up. Another important contemporary issue, the plight of prisoners of conscience, is the subject of a medal by Ian Rank-Broadley (60). But medals also record the more mundane aspects of modern life. *Greetings from King's Cross*, a medallic postcard by Danuta Solowiej, a Polish-born artist living in London, focusses on underground commuting (91), whilst John Paddison's **Monday Morning** (134) celebrates washing day.

87

60

91

134

34

Since the earliest medals of Renaissance Italy, the portrait has been a principal feature of medallic design. The architect **Frank Lloyd Wright** is portrayed by American artist John Cook (34). A medal of **Virginia Woolf** by Cook's compatriot Leonda Finke has a reverse that refers to Woolf's book, *A Room of One's Own*, and to an artist's need for independent space in which to work (59). The poet **Dylan Thomas** is the subject of a medal by Welsh sculptor Jonah Jones (28), and Dutch medal curator **Gay van der Meer** of another by Geer Steyn (74). The portrait of **Elisabeth Frink** by Avril Vaughan (93) was approved by the sculptor before her death in 1993. Philip Nathan's medal of **Turner** has a reverse that brilliantly evokes the painter's work (65).

59

28

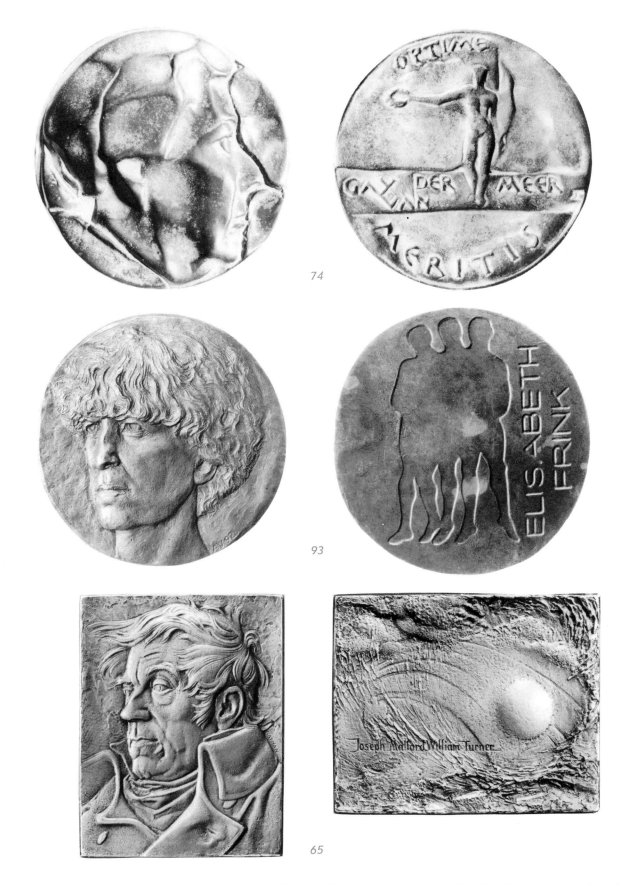

74

93

65

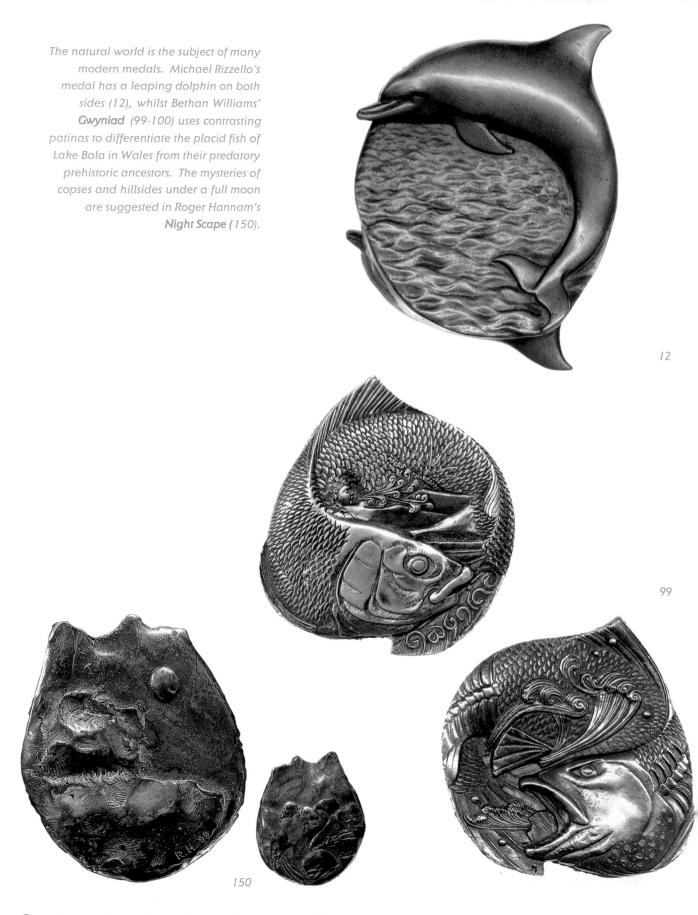

The natural world is the subject of many modern medals. Michael Rizzello's medal has a leaping dolphin on both sides (12), whilst Bethan Williams' **Gwyniad** (99-100) uses contrasting patinas to differentiate the placid fish of Lake Bala in Wales from their predatory prehistoric ancestors. The mysteries of copses and hillsides under a full moon are suggested in Roger Hannam's **Night Scape** (150).

12

99

150

Human interventions in the landscape also provide medallists with material. The inscription on Ron Dutton's **Stonehenge** *(46)* reads: 'Stones unencumbered by priest ritual chant Stand sadly posed upon untrodden grass A monument to faded hope and spirits passed'. The exterior and interior of the ruined Linlithgow Palace, birthplace of Mary queen of Scots, are evoked in **Linlithgow Threshold** by Simon Beeson *(159)* - the threshold links the two sides of the wall-like medal.

46

159

Myths and legends are fertile sources of inspiration. The two-sidedness of the medal is exploited in Geoffrey Clarke's **Pyramus and Thisbe** (32), with the medal itself becoming the wall through which the lovers speak. Two of Aesop's fables, *The fox and grapes* and *The fox and crow*, were the sources for a medal by Julian Cross (95). Linda Crook's **Leda and the Hat-pin** (141) subverts an ancient Greek legend: in this version Leda has made the swan (Zeus) into an elaborate hat, which she impales with a hat-pin. Nicola Moss's **George and the Dragon** (40) is a modern reworking of another legend - on the back the princess crops her hair prior to rescuing herself!

32

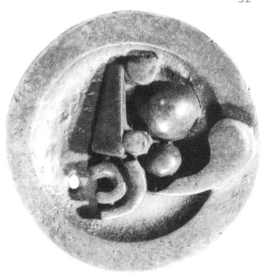

95

141

40

31

The diversity of medallic subjects is indicated here. Joan Thompson's **Pisces** (31) uses the medium's expressive possibilities to the full: the watery subject is echoed in the medal's pebble-like form. Marian Fountain's **The Muse and the Mother** (72) is a metaphor of two states of womanhood. A poem by Verlaine and the pyramids of Egypt are the inspiration behind the other medals - by Gerald Laing (98) and Guy Richardson (108) respectively.

72

ET O CES VOIX D'ENFANTS CHANTANT DANS LA COUPOLE

LE VASE PUR OU RESPLENDIT LE SANG REEL · IL ADORE GLOIRE ET SYMBOLE ET

98

108

5 Medals in the 21st century: the BAMS Student Medal Project

It is self-evident that the long-term future of the medal as an art form in Britain must depend upon it attracting the interest of those young artists who are now attending art colleges up and down the country.

Conversely, art students themselves have much to gain from making medals. This point has been underlined by Bryan Kneale, RA, who, as professor at the Royal Academy schools, maintained that, 'one of the most interesting things as far as students are concerned is that this is a very good introduction to bronze casting as a way of making sculpture. It's not daunting because of the scale, and I think every student should try it. I've seen again and again students who I wouldn't have associated with modelling at all actually produce something really extraordinary. It may reveal some completely new territory, and after all that's one of the things that artists are about; it's a process of constant renewal and any technical problem is often the way through to much greater things.'

In the 1980s the Royal Society of Arts encouraged art students to develop an interest in the subject by organising an annual medal competition, for which the prizes took the form of travel bursaries; this scheme was later taken over by the Royal Society of British Sculptors (RBS). In a separate initiative and with the assistance of the Royal Mint, the Royal College of Art instituted its own annual medal course, also with an associated competition. The RBS competitions ceased in the mid 1990s, but by this time BAMS had founded its annual Student Medal Project, with the intention of bringing medal-making and casting into the curricula of greater numbers of art colleges.

Under the BAMS initiative, which in 2003 celebrates its tenth anniversary, students are introduced to the medal, in both its historical and contemporary manifestations, and then go on to produce a medal of their own. These medals are cast in the college foundries, and are then entered into a competition organised by BAMS. Several prizes are awarded each year, and a catalogue is produced in which each medal is discussed and the prize-winners illustrated; the winning medals often also feature in the society's journal, *The Medal*. Many of the medals are shown in a

58 touring exhibition, with past venues including the Yorkshire Museum, York, Pallant

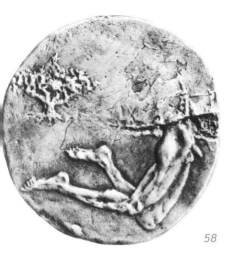

58

House Gallery, Chichester, the Vision Centre, Cork, and also a commercial space: Simmons Gallery in London's Lamb's Conduit Street. BAMS has also included some of the medals in Royal Academy summer shows and in FIDEM exhibitions abroad. A number of the winners of the grand prize have subsequently been commissioned to make a medal for BAMS, whilst on other occasions the winning medal has been issued by the society on the same terms as those medals produced by more experienced artists.

The project is welcomed by college tutors, for it allows their students to focus on a defined project within a specific discipline - with all the restrictions and possibilities that that entails - and to carry a piece of work through from beginning to end, from the design stage, through the modelling, to the final casting and finishing. It also gives the students experience of exhibiting their work, and, given that the medals can be produced in editions, of selling it. In all, the project offers invaluable experience to the young artists involved, and has been found to fit well into degree courses at all three years, as well as at postgraduate level. In the context of the 1996 Student Medal Project, its organiser, BAMS secretary Marcy Leavitt Bourne, wrote that, 'for students and teachers alike, the medal proved to be a medium in which exploration, experimentation and occasionally surprise all played their part'. In the catalogue of the 2001 exhibition, the same writer explained: 'The Student Medal Project exists to encourage student initiative and nurture enthusiasm. It aims to revitalise the medal, maintaining the links to its Renaissance origins but grafting it securely to the contemporary curriculum of art colleges, thereby ensuring it a voice in the language of today's art.'

In the 1980s BAMS commissioned a number of medals from winners of the Royal Society of Arts student medal competitions. These included Annabel Eley's **Carnival** *(6) and Gordon Summers'* **The Pursuit of Knowledge** *(58), in which the figure's lust for knowledge draws him through the body of the medal.*

The tutors are also encouraged to make medals, and these are exhibited alongside the student work, and appear in the catalogue (but are not entered into the competition). Like the students, the tutors may not have considered medals before, but often find that the demands of the medal take them in new directions and help develop their other work.

The success of the project is indicated by the number of colleges that have been

6

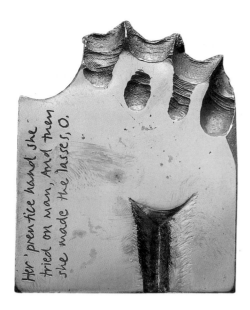

involved, most of them for many years. They are: Birmingham Institute of Art and Design, University of Central England; Carmarthenshire College of Technology and Art; Central St Martin's College of Art and Design; Chelsea College of Art and Design; Crawford College of Art and Design, Cork; Duncan of Jordanstone College of Art and Design; Edinburgh College of Art; Falmouth College of Arts; Glasgow School of Art; Kingston University, School of Fine Art; Loughborough University School of Art and Design; Norwich School of Art and Design; Sheffield Hallam University; Stafford College of Arts and Technology; Wimbledon School of Art; and University of Wolverhampton, School of Art and Design. A number of colleges from other countries have also participated.

Over the years the project has benefited from the support of many sponsors. These have included Alec Tiranti Ltd, The Art Bronze Foundry, The Bigbury Mint, The Birmingham Mint Ltd, Bonhams, Dr Joan Fitzgerald, Galata Print Ltd, The Goldsmiths' Company, John Donald Designer Goldsmith, London Metal Exchange, Lunts Casting Ltd, Nautilus Fine Art Foundry, Niagara Falls Castings Ltd, Pangolin Editions, The Royal Mint, Sotheby's, Spink & Son, Theo Fennell plc, Thomas Fattorini Ltd, The Worshipful Company of Cutlers, The Worshipful Company of Founders, and a number of anonymous benefactors. Without the enlightened generosity of these institutions and individuals this important initiative would not be able to continue.

122

124

Hazel White won a prize for her medal while studying at the Royal College of Art. Her subsequent BAMS medal, **And Then She Made the Lasses, O** (122), quotes from Robert Burns. The other medals illustrated here are by winners of the BAMS Student Medal Project. Dana Krinsky was a student at Central St Martin's College of Art and Design when she won a prize in 1996; her BAMS medal, **Walking** (124), is concerned with life and the choices we all make without knowing the consequences. Jane Sedgwick's **Isolate** (136) was born of a love of modern architecture, the medal's changing perspectives and contrasts of light and dark mirroring our experiences of interior spaces. **Sleeping Tablet** by Carole Dodds (153) takes the form of a pillow, but also of an ancient Babylonian tablet, and incorporates a child's drawing and a text in mirror-writing. **Dreams of a Dying Moth** by Lucy Willow, a student at Falmouth College of Arts (158), won the Project's top prize in 2001, and was issued by BAMS the following year.

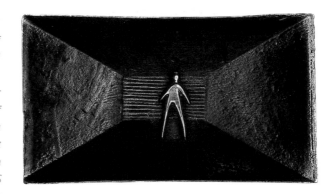

136

153

158

6 Commissioning a medal: celebration and reward

BAMS commissions several medals each year, but medals are also commissioned for their own use by individuals, colleges, companies, and many other types of organisation. Whether mementoes or awards, they are always treasured.

For many, commissioning a medal is a new experience, but for some institutions it is a long tradition. All Souls College, Oxford, for example, issues a medal to mark the turning of each century and the accompanying college ceremony of 'hunting the mallard'. For its medal for 2000, the college chose to work with artist Jane McAdam Freud. According to senior dean, Jeremy Lever, QC, 'The commissioning of the medal on this occasion was a stimulating and exciting experience; and the resulting medal, designed by Jane McAdam Freud and struck by the Bigbury Mint, has been universally admired for its beauty and historical symbolism.' The Royal Asiatic Society also has a long history of commissioning medals, and saw the new millennium as an appropriate moment to begin a new series of awards in the form of cast medals. At the conclusion of the process the society's director, Rachel Ward, was able to write: 'We are thrilled with the new medal by Danuta Solowiej, which is inspired by designs made in 1823 by Thomas and William Daniell, members of the Royal Asiatic Society famous for their views of India.' Similar enriching experiences are open to all, for commissioning a medal is a simple enough matter, but it is important to approach it in a way that ensures that the exercise is smooth-running and the final medal is admired by all those involved.

It is vital both that enough time is allowed (the process can take several months) and that sufficient funds are set aside to cover the production costs. If the commissioner is an organisation, it will be advisable for one or two trusted individuals within the organisation to be appointed to oversee the process, liaise with the artist, and agree the design: decision by committee will almost certainly cause delays and disagreements, and be detrimental to the finished medal. If required, BAMS will provide advice on how best to proceed and assistance in identifying a suitable artist. Certain of the medal dealers also offer this service, and will act as an intermediary between commissioner and artist.

The commissioner will need to decide first of all what function the medal is intended to serve, for this will determine both how many examples are required, and also, by implication, what will be the more appropriate production method: striking or casting. Making dies from which to strike a medal is a time-consuming and expensive process, but striking the individual medals is relatively cheap. Casting does not require dies, but the production of each medal is more labour-intensive, and therefore more costly. Striking is therefore generally more suited to larger editions, and casting to smaller numbers.

Thought should also be given to the metal in which the medal will be produced. The traditional metals for medals are gold, silver and bronze (a term denoting an alloy of copper and tin, but also used more generally in the medallic context to cover any copper alloy). Bronze is often preferred to precious metals, for it has enormous potential in terms of variety of finish and patination, which can greatly enhance the design. It is also less expensive, and, as the Royal Asiatic Society noted when commissioning its recent medal, 'it was felt that the recipient might prefer a less valuable material which he/she could leave out on his/her desk to be handled and admired rather than hidden away in a safe'.

Most importantly, the commissioner will also need to select an artist (who will probably be able to advise on the best method of production). The artist will be someone whose previous work appeals. It may be that in the first instance two or more artists will be approached, in order to identify one who is both able and willing to undertake the work, and to ascertain the fee that would be involved. However, an artist's time is (like everybody's) valuable, and so a request for ideas or drawings should generally be made only after the commission has been granted and payment promised. Most artists prefer to be commissioned directly, but if the commissioner prefers to ask for drawings from more than one artist, it should be remembered that this will increase the costs, and it is important to inform each artist that the commission is taking the form of a limited competition. Competitions may give the commissioner more overall choice, but they can also have disadvantages. They may act as a brake on the development of a personal relationship between commissioner and artist, and they can also delay crucial discussions concerning the design.

Jane McAdam Freud's struck medal for All Souls College, Oxford (left), has a commemorative function. The male and female mallard allude both to an ancient college ceremony and to the admission of women as fellows in the twentieth century, whilst the reverse is based on a sundial designed for the college by Christopher Wren. By contrast, the Royal Asiatic Society cast medal, by Danuta Solowiej (below), serves as an award; its reverse features the vast rooting branches of the banyan tree.

Most artists will welcome suggestions as to what imagery might be appropriate for the medal, and background information relating to the commission and the organisation or individual placing it will also be useful. But the best results are invariably gained by giving the artist as free a range as possible in producing a design. Insisting on the inclusion of a logo, for example, can present difficulties, and it is also advisable to keep to a minimum the number of words required on the medal. In the first instance the artist may be asked to produce rough sketches, which can then be discussed with the commissioner. Once a general scheme has been decided upon, the artist may be asked for a finished drawing. Once this is approved, he or she will go on to produce a model, which may be in wax, clay, plaster, or some other material. This model will then be approved by the commissioner.

If the medal is to be cast - which is the more usual production technique when fewer than, say, one hundred examples are required - the artist's model will be the same size as the finished medals. The artist will arrange for a mould to be taken from this model, from which further models in wax may be taken; the medals will then be cast at a foundry from these waxes, using what is known as the lost wax technique. Alternatively, but less commonly, each side of the artist's model can be impressed into boxes of cohesive sand, which, when brought together, leave a space that can be filled with molten metal; this is known as sand-casting. Whichever of these two casting processes is used, the artist will then generally finish and patinate the medals.

If the medal is to be struck - which is more usual if many more than around one hundred medals are wanted - the model will generally be of a larger size than the finished medals. The artist will arrange for the model to be sent to a mint, where dies will be produced using a pantographic device known as a reducing machine. An alternative procedure is for the artist to dispense with the model and produce the designs by engraving directly into the dies; this was a common practice before the invention of the reducing machine, but is not greatly used nowadays. The dies are always the same size as the finished medals, and it is from them that the medals are struck.

To summarise, costs for cast medals will therefore generally comprise: the artist's drawing, the artist's model, the making of a mould, the making of waxes, the casting of the medals, and the finishing and patination. Costs for struck medals will comprise: the artist's drawing, the artist's model, the making of the dies by the reducing process, and the striking of the medals. There may also be a cost for packaging, about which the artist will be able to advise.

Medal commissions vary enormously in their size. At one end of the scale medals can form an integral feature of public art projects. As a result of a recent scheme for Kielder Forest, devised by artist Nicola Moss and funded by a partnership of Northumbrian Water, Forest Enterprise, the Northumberland Tourist Board and Northern Arts, visitors to the forest can take home with them a keepsake medal, along with a book of rubbings that they make from a series of twelve bronze reliefs placed along their walk. Public art is generally monolithic, but in this case the work is fragmented, and individuals become directly involved, producing their own book, and taking away a memento of their visit. The medal helps to bridge the gap between public and personal, and the success of the project has led to similar initiatives being established elsewhere.

Other commissions, such as those placed by All Souls College and the Royal Asiatic Society cited above, are designed for more private use, within the commissioning body. Others are of a still more wholly personal nature. The potential rewards of these are articulated by the commissioner of the wedding anniversary medal illustrated here, another commission from Nicola Moss, for which London's Simmons Gallery acted as advisors: 'It was a wonderful experience. We learned much about ourselves, about each other and our lives and family, about the artist's need to both communicate and remain inviolate, working at her own pace in her own visual or rather tactile realm. And we feel privileged to have been the means of enriching the world by an object whose modest size keeps blossoming into layers upon layers of meaning.'

This medal by Nicola Moss was a private commission, intended as a gift to family members in celebration of a golden wedding anniversary. Without words or dates, the medal contains subtle allusions to fifty shared years.

SOME USEFUL TERMS

BAMS.   The British Art Medal Society, founded in 1982.

casting.   A process for making medals, in which molten metal is poured into a space formerly occupied by a model (q.v.).

die.   A metal stamp, usually cylindrical and made of steel, from which struck medals are produced.

edition.   The number of examples of a medal produced. Striking (q.v.) is generally used for larger editions; casting (q.v.) for smaller.

engraving.   The process of cutting an image into a die, either by use of a reducing machine (q.v.) or by hand. A mould (q.v.) may also be engraved.

exergue.   The segmental area at the bottom of more traditional medal designs. On coins, the year sometimes appears in this space.

FIDEM.   The Fédération Internationale de la Médaille (International Medal Federation), founded in 1937. It organises biennial exhibitions of contemporary medals, each of which is held in a different venue around the world. BAMS is affiliated to FIDEM.

finishing.   The process of working on a cast medal to remove imperfections left by the casting process.

foundry.   An establishment for casting medals and other objects in metal.

medallist.   An artist who makes medals.

mint.   An establishment for striking medals and coins.

model.   The original piece on which an artist has worked to produce a medal, it may be made of any of a wide range of materials. Also, a wax piece produced from a mould (q.v.) for casting.

mould.   An impression, often in plaster, taken from a model, into which details, such as lettering, may be engraved; an impression may then in turn be taken of the mould, and worked on further. Moulds, now often made of rubber, are also used to produce wax models for casting.

obverse.   The front of a medal.

patinating.   The process of colouring a cast medal, generally by heating and applying chemicals.

reducing machine.   A pantographic device, used for translating an artist's model (q.v.) into a die (q.v.).

reverse.   The back of a medal.

striking.   A process for making medals, in which two dies (q.v.) are brought to bear on a blank piece of metal. This process is also used for making coins.

CONTACTS

For information about membership of the British Art Medal Society, contact Peter Bagwell Purefoy on 01892 613370; peter@purefoy.fsnet.co.uk

For information about the BAMS Student Medal Project, contact Marcy Leavitt Bourne on 020-7794 9703; eobourne@aol.com

For general enquiries about BAMS and advice on commissioning medals, contact Philip Attwood on 020-7323 8260; pattwood@thebritishmuseum.ac.uk

Alternatively, write to BAMS, c/o Department of Coins and Medals, British Museum, London WC1B 3DG.

READING ABOUT MEDALS

The best general introduction to the subject is Mark Jones' *The art of the medal* (London: British Museum Publications, 1979). The book is out of print, but is readily available from sellers of second-hand books on the internet.

The Medal, the journal of the British Art Medal Society, is published by the British Art Medal Trust (BAMT), and appears twice a year. Essential reading for anyone interested in medals, it covers the Renaissance to the present, and enables the reader to build up a knowledge of all aspects of medallic art. Indexes are published every five years, to provide easy reference. Back issues are available.

Various books published by BAMT allow the reader to focus on specific topics. *Designs on posterity: drawings for medals*, edited by Mark Jones, is a collection of essays examining the relationship between drawing and medals from the Italian Renaissance to German Expressionism. *The Pingo family and medal making in 18th-century Britain*, by Christopher Eimer, traces five generations of a family that produced a number of celebrated medallists, and contains a catalogue of all their known work.

Luke Syson's *size immaterial: hand-held sculpture of the 1990s* was published by BAMT to coincide with a British Museum exhibition of some of the best contemporary medals of recent years, and includes a discussion of the most innovative pieces from around the world. Catalogues of past BAMS Student Medal Project exhibitions are also available.

To order BAMT publications, contact Galata, The Old White Lion, Market Street, Llanfyllin, Powys SY22 5BX, Great Britain; e-mail Paul@galata.co.uk.

SPONSORS

Dix Noonan Webb are specialist auctioneers and valuers of all types of coins, medals and paper money. Established in London since 1990, the company boasts over 150 years' combined experience in numismatics, and has staged over ninety auctions. We pride ourselves in providing an unpretentious, friendly service to clients, and warmly welcome enquiries from all those wishing to buy or sell at auction.

Since 1993 historical and art medals have featured in virtually every DNW coin auction. Today, we are the world's pre-eminent auctioneers of art medals, offering a wide and varied range in each catalogue to suit all collecting tastes. A full record of every historical and art medal sold by DNW can be found on our website, www.dnw.co.uk. The database is searchable by a number of criteria, including artist, subject and year. In addition, the site features a fully illustrated account of the development of the art medal. The website contains details of medals in forthcoming auctions, with details posted on the site as the cataloguing for each auction progresses. All illustrations can be viewed as colour enlargements.

Dix Noonan Webb are proud to be associated with the British Art Medal Society and fully support the endeavours of the Society to bring the subject of the medal to a wider audience.

BAMS MEDALS 1982 - 2002

We list here all the medals issued by the British Art Medal Society during its first twenty years.

1. PICASSO
by Jane McAdam Freud, 1981.
Cast bronze. 90 x 80mm. Cast by the Royal
Mint. *The Medal*, no. 1 (1982). Edition: 35.

2. MUSE
by Mark Holloway, 1982.
Cast bronze. 70 x 50mm. Cast by Lunt.
The Medal, no. 1 (1982). Edition: 12.

3. FOOD FURROWS
by Jacqueline Stieger, 1982.
Cast bronze. 65mm. *The Medal*, no. 1
(1982). Edition: 24.

4. SHEEP MOOR II
by Ron Dutton, 1982.
Cast bronze. 78mm. *The Medal*, no. 1
(1982). Edition: 33.

5. BRONZE SHOAL
by Nigel Hall, 1982.
Cast bronze. 79mm. *The Medal*, no. 1
(1982). Edition: 21.

6. CARNIVAL
by Annabel Eley, 1982.
Cast bronze, 76 x 93mm. *The Medal*, no. 2
(1983). Edition: 29.

7. GRACE DARLING
by Robert Elderton, 1983.
Cast bronze. 90mm. *The Medal*, no. 2
(1983). Edition: 47.

8. TURNING CIRCLE
by John Maine, 1983.
Struck bronze. 60mm. Struck by Fattorini.
The Medal, no. 2 (1983). Edition: 38.

9. THE HORRORS OF WAR
by Malcolm Appleby, 1983.
Cast bronze. 47 x 55mm. *The Medal*, no. 3
(1983). Edition: 25.

10. OSPREY
by Fred Rich, 1983.
Cast bronze, gilt and enamelled. 70 x
62mm. Cast by Lunt. *The Medal*, no. 3
(1983). Edition: 60.

11. CHARLES DICKENS
by Ronald Searle, 1983.
Struck bronze. 71mm. Struck by the
Birmingham Mint. *The Medal*, no. 4 (1984).
Edition: 100.

12. DOLPHIN
by Michael Rizzello, 1983.
Cast Bronze. 90mm. Cast by Lunt. *The Medal*,
no. 4 (1984). Edition: 71.

13. LORD OLIVIER
by Fred Kormis, 1983.
Cast bronze. 115mm. *The Medal*, no. 4
(1984). Edition: 19.

14. JOHN SCHLESINGER
by Fred Kormis, 1983.
Cast bronze. 115mm. Cast by Lunt.
The Medal, no. 4 (1984). Edition: 17.

15. TERROR/VIRTUE
by Ian Hamilton Finlay, 1983.
Cast bronze. 52.5mm. Cast by Lunt.
The Medal, no. 4 (1984). Edition: 43 plus
a number sold by the artist.

16. THEATRE
by Cecilia Leete, 1983.
Cast bronze. 75 x 57mm. Cast by Lunt.
The Medal, no. 4 (1984). Edition: 21.

17. RENÉ MAGRITTE
by Laurence Burt, 1983.
Cast bronze. 77mm. Cast by Lunt.
The Medal, no. 4 (1984). Edition: 30.

18. DIAMOND
by Lynn Chadwick, 1983.
Struck bronze. 76mm. *The Medal*, no. 5
(1984). Edition: 128.

19. MICHELANGELO
by Frank Forster, 1984.
Cast bronze. 94mm. Cast by the artist.
The Medal, no. 5 (1984). Edition: 35.

20. SAMUEL PEPYS
by Ronald Searle, 1984.
Struck bronze. 70mm. Struck by the
Birmingham Mint. *The Medal*, no. 6 (1985).
Edition: 93.

21. HEAD
by János Kalmár, 1984.
Cast bronze. 97 x 66mm. *The Medal*, no. 6
(1985). Edition: 28.

22. JOHN BETJEMAN
by Peter Quinn, 1985.
Cast bronze. 105mm. Cast by Lunt.
The Medal, no. 6 (1985). Edition: 47.

23. REASON VERSUS PLEASURE
by Carl Plackman, 1985.
Cast bronze. 108mm. Cast by Lunt.
The Medal, no. 6 (1985). Edition: 18.

24. MONUMENTA
by Marian Fountain, 1985.
Cast bronze. 68 x 40mm. Cast by the artist.
The Medal, no. 6 (1985). Edition: 37.

25. TURNING CIRCLE
by John Maine.
Struck silver. 60mm. *The Medal*, no. 7
(1985). Edition: 10.

26. CHARLES DICKENS
by Ronald Searle.
Uniface bust, cast bronze. 250mm.
The Medal, no. 7 (1985). Edition: 6.

27. CHARLES DICKENS
by Ronald Searle.
Uniface reverse, cast bronze. 250mm.
The Medal, no. 7 (1985). Edition: 6.

28. DYLAN THOMAS
by Jonah Jones, 1985.
Cast bronze. 125mm. Cast in sand by
Hogans. *The Medal*, no. 7 (1985).
Edition: 37.

29. GALA
by Lloyd Carter, 1985.
Cast bronze. 108mm. *The Medal*, no. 7
(1985). Edition: 26.

30. PERILLUS PHALARIS
by David Renka, 1985.
Cast bronze. 75.5mm. *The Medal*, no. 7
(1985). Edition: 24.

31. PISCES
by Joan Thompson, 1985.
Cast bronze. 69mm. Cast by RED Bronze.
The Medal, no. 7 (1985). Edition: 26.

32. PYRAMUS AND THISBE
by Geoffrey Clarke, 1985.
Cast bronze. 90mm. Cast at Wolverhampton
Polytechnic. *The Medal*, no. 7 (1985).
Edition: 38.

33. A TREE FOR ME
by Ronald Pennell, 1985.
Cast bronze. Obverse engraved on a glass
lens, from which moulds were taken and
medals cast in silver; the reverse carved on
the silver medal, which then served as a
master from which moulds were taken.
48mm. *The Medal*, no. 7 (1985). Edition: 28.

34. FRANK LLOYD WRIGHT
by John Cook, 1985.
Cast bronze. 85 x 88mm. *The Medal*, no. 8
(1986). Edition: 64.

35. BERNINI GETTING THE MESSAGE FROM
THE ANGEL OF THE BAROQUE
by Ronald Searle, 1985.
Struck bronze. 70mm. Struck by the Pobjoy
Mint. *The Medal*, no. 8 (1986). Edition: 40.

36. TEN YEARS OF HYPHEN
by Paul Neagu, 1985/6.
Cast bronze. 100mm. *The Medal*, no. 8
(1986). Edition: 17.

37. FALL OUT
by Malcolm Appleby, 1986.
Struck silver. 29mm. Struck by the artist from
hand-engraved dies. *The Medal*, no. 10
(1986). Edition: 39.

38. CANNIBAL MEDAL
by Ronald Searle, 1986.
Cast bronze. 108mm. *The Medal*, no. 10
(1986). Edition: 21.

39. BELGRANO MEDAL - A MEDAL OF
DISHONOUR
by Michael Sandle, 1986.
Cast bronze. 81.5mm. *The Medal*, no. 10
(1986). Edition: 56.

40. GEORGE AND THE DRAGON
by Nicola Moss, 1986.
Cast bronze. 116 x 103mm. Partly carved
intaglio in marble, partly modelled in wax.
Cast at High Wycombe and finished by the
artist. *The Medal*, no. 10 (1986). Edition: 96.

41. TICKET TO AUDNAX
by Hilary Oliver, 1986.
Cast bronze. 89mm. *The Medal*, no. 10
(1986). Edition: 12.

42. APHRODITE HANGING OUT HER
WASHING IN AKROTIRI IS FRIGHTENED BY A
SNAKE/ A SNAKE IS FRIGHTENED BY
APHRODITE AS SHE HANGS OUT HER
WASHING IN AKROTIRI
by Peter Welton, 1986.
Cast bronze. 91mm. *The Medal*, no. 10
(1986). Edition: 22.

43. WALK THROUGH SENANQUES
by Caroline White, 1986.
Cast bronze. 120mm. *The Medal*, no. 10
(1986). Edition: 20.

44. BOGMAN
by Carole Hodgson, 1987.
Cast bronze. 79mm. *The Medal*, no. 11
(1987). Edition: 24.

45. THE JAMES MONAHAN MEDAL
by Kevin Coates, 1987.
Cast bronze. 50 x 52mm. *The Medal*, no. 11
(1987). Edition: 27 plus those awarded.

46. STONEHENGE
by Ron Dutton, 1987.
Cast bronze. 97mm. *The Medal*, no. 11
(1987). Edition: 70.

47. BOTTOM
by Barry Hopewell, 1997.
Cast bronze. 109mm. *The Medal*, no. 11
(1987). Edition: 16.

48. DREAMER
by John Paddison, 1987.
Cast bronze. 97mm. *The Medal*, no. 11
(1987). Edition: 20.

49. IN PRAISE OF LIMESTONE
by Derek Morris, 1987.
Cast bronze. 96mm. *The Medal*, no. 12
(1988). Edition: 32.

50. DIARY
by José Aurelio, 1987
Cast bronze. 77mm. *The Medal*, no. 13
(1988). Edition: 31.

51. COVE AND BEACH
by Paul Mason, 1988.
Cast bronze. 88mm. *The Medal*, no. 13
(1988). Edition: 26.

52. MAYA MEDALLION - THE DARK ONE
by Dhruva Mistry, 1988.
Cast bronze. 133mm. *The Medal*, no. 13
(1988). Edition: 56.

53. BATTLE OF BRITAIN
by Michael Meszaros, 1988.
Cast bronze. 110mm. *The Medal*, no. 13
(1988). Edition: 30.

54. SAINT GAUDENS/ EAKINS
by Leonard Baskin, 1988.
Struck bronze. 60mm. Struck by Fattorini.
The Medal, no. 13 (1988). Edition: 50.

55. ATHENA AND ME
by Avril Vaughan, 1988.
Cast bronze. 76mm. The obverse cut intaglio
into plaster; the reverse modelled in wax.
The Medal, no. 14 (1989). Edition: 57.

56. BROWSING ON THE WORLD TREE
by Deborah Ward, 1988.
Cast bronze. 80 x 50mm. *The Medal*, no. 14
(1989). Edition: 20.

57. THE CRUEL OCEAN
by Ivanka Mincheva, 1988.
Cast bronze. 98mm. *The Medal*, no. 14
(1989). Edition: 22.

58. THE FRUIT OF KNOWLEDGE
by Gordon Summers, 1989.
Cast bronze. 68mm. *The Medal*, no. 14
(1989). Edition: 27.

59. VIRGINIA WOOLF - A ROOM OF ONE'S
OWN
by Leonda Finke, 1989.
Cast bronze. 94 x 79mm. *The Medal*, no. 15
(1989). Edition: 63.

60. PRISONER OF CONSCIENCE
by Ian Rank-Broadley, 1989.
Cast bronze. 120mm. Cast by the Royal Mint.
The Medal, no. 15 (1989). Edition: 85.

61. SISYPHUS
by Jane McAdam Freud, 1989.
Cast bronze. 90 x 100mm. Cast by the Royal
Mint. *The Medal*, no. 16 (1990). Edition: 60.

62. ACTA EST FABULA
by Bogomil Nikolov, 1989.
Cast bronze. 110mm. Cast by Tallix Morris
Singer. *The Medal*, no. 16 (1990).
Edition: 24.

63. OSCAR WILDE
by Danuta Solowiej, 1989.
Cast bronze. 101 x 75mm. Cast in sand by
the artist. *The Medal*, no. 16 (1990).
Edition: 18.

64. MOONSCAPE
by Bud Wertheim, 1989.
Cast bronze. 80 x 80mm. Cast by Tallix
Morris Singer. *The Medal*, no. 16 (1990).
Edition: 14.

65. TURNER
by Philip Nathan, 1989.
Cast bronze. 110 x 87mm. Cast by the Royal
Mint. *The Medal*, no. 16 (1990). Edition: 42.

66. HOMAGE TO COLLECTORS
by John Lobban, 1990.
Cast bronze. 100mm. Cast in silver, engraved
and chased in the metal, and subsequently
cast in bronze by Tallix Morris Singer and the
Royal Mint. *The Medal*, no. 17 (1990).
Edition: 85.

67. SEARLE AT SEVENTY
by Ronald Searle, 1990.
Struck bronze, silver plated. 70mm. Struck
by Fattorini. 70mm. *The Medal*, no. 17
(1990). Edition: 80.

68. WAVE AND SPINDRIFT HIGHER THAN
THE MAST
by Frances Pelly, 1990.
Cast bronze. 90 x 65mm. Cast by Tallix
Morris Singer. *The Medal*, no. 17 (1990).
Edition: 14.

69. WOLFGANG AMADEUS MOZART
by Kevin Coates, 1990.
Cast silver. 60 x 51mm. *The Medal*, no. 18
(1991). Edition: 40.

70. HAEC UBI REGNANT
by David Chandler, 1990.
Cast bronze. 103mm. *The Medal*, no. 18
(1991). Edition: 21.

71. GOOD NIGHT, GOOD MORNING
by Peter Ellis, 1990.
Cast bronze. 115mm. *The Medal*, no. 18
(1991). Edition: 16.

72. THE MUSE AND THE MOTHER
by Marian Fountain, 1990.
Cast bronze with some gilding. 98 x 115mm.
The Medal, no. 18 (1991). Edition: 42.

73. SAVE OUR AIR EARTH WATER
by Berndt Helleberg, 1990.
Cast bronze. 96mm. *The Medal*, no. 19
(1991). Edition: 15.

74. GAY VAN DER MEER
by Geer Steyn, 1991.
Cast bronze. 86mm. *The Medal*, no. 19
(1991). Edition: 50.

75. SUMMER
by Irene Gunston, 1991.
Cast bronze. 101 x 88mm. *The Medal*, no. 19
(1991). Edition: 20.

76. A BOOK OF LEAVES
by Rob Kesseler, 1991.
Cast bronze. 70 x 78mm. *The Medal*, no. 19
(1991). Edition: 24.

77. THE MAN WHO PLANTED TREES
by Nicola Moss, 1991.
Cast bronze. 68mm. *The Medal*, no. 19
(1991). Edition: 30.

78. KWAI 50TH ANNIVERSARY MEDAL
by Ronald Searle, 1991.
Struck bronze. 70mm. Struck by Fattorini.
The Medal, no. 20 (1992). Edition: 100.

79. BYE BYE EYE
by Ronald Searle, 1991.
Cast bronze. 65 x 90mm. Cast by Tallix
Morris Singer. *The Medal*, no. 20 (1992).
Edition: 25.

80. THE PARMA
by Malcolm Appleby, 1991.
Cast silver. 67 x 60mm. Cast by Niagara Falls.
The Medal, no. 20 (1992). Edition: 24.

81. THE PARMA
by Malcolm Appleby, 1991.
Cast bronze. 67 x 60mm. Cast by Niagara
Falls. *The Medal*, no. 20 (1992). Edition: 32.

82. MEDAL LOVER
by Robin Ashby, 1991.
Cast bronze. 86 x 87mm. Cast by Tallix
Morris Singer. *The Medal*, no. 20 (1992).
Edition: 30.

83. ICARUS TRIES
by Ron Dutton, 1991.
Cast bronze. 90mm. Cast by the artist. *The
Medal*, no. 20 (1992). Edition: 27.

84. MEDAL FOR DALI
by Simon Ward, 1991.
Cast bronze. 84mm. Cast by Tallix Morris
Singer. *The Medal*, no. 20 (1992).
Edition: 18.

85. EPIDAUROS
by Werner Niermann, 1991.
Cast bronze. 95 x 110mm. Cast by the artist.
The Medal, no. 21 (1992). Edition: 37.

86. RECORD OF MEMORY
by Eva Wilson, 1992.
Cast bronze. 100 x 70mm. Cast by
Powderhall Bronze. *The Medal*, no. 21
(1992). Edition: 25.

87. DESTRUCTION OF THE TOWN
by Jacqueline Stieger, 1992.
Cast bronze. 74mm. Cast by Niagara Falls.
The Medal, no. 21 (1992). Edition: 24.

88. HALF BAKED
by Lucian Taylor, 1992.
Cast bronze. 68 x 35 x 13mm. Cast by
Powderhall Bronze. *The Medal*, no. 21
(1992). Edition: 11.

89. A MEDAL FOR BAMS
by Marián Polonsky, 1992.
Cast bronze. 118mm. *The Medal*, no. 21
(1992). Edition: 32.

90. A BIRD IN THE HAND IS WORTH TWO IN
THE BUSH - BUT WILL THEY SURVIVE?
By Ronald Pennell, 1992.
Cast bronze. 95mm. Cast by Lunt.
The Medal, no. 22 (1993). Edition: 15.

91. GREETINGS FROM KING'S CROSS
by Danuta Solowiej, 1992.
Cast bronze. 105 x 150mm. Cast by the
artist. *The Medal*, no. 22 (1993). Edition: 22.

92. BITE BACK
by Linda Crook, 1992.
Cast bronze. 97mm. Cast by Bronze Age.
The Medal, no. 22 (1993). Edition: 29.

93. ELISABETH FRINK
by Avril Vaughan, 1992.
Cast bronze. 98mm. Cast by the Royal Mint.
The Medal, no. 23 (1993). Edition: 47.

94. OF MADNESS AND MEMORY
by Gordon Summers, 1992.
Cast bronze. 58mm. Cast by Powderhall
Bronze. *The Medal*, no. 23 (1993).
Edition: 10.

95. FOX AND GRAPES AND CROW
by Julian Cross, 1993.
Cast bronze. 87 x 80mm. Cast by Niagara
Falls. *The Medal*, no. 23 (1993). Edition: 47.

96. ASTERIX AND OBELIX
by Sandeha Lynch, 1993.
Cast bronze. 74mm. *The Medal*, no. 24
(1994). Edition: 36.

97. EASTERN EUROPE
By Enikő Szöllőssy, 1991.
Cast bronze. 120mm. *The Medal*, no. 24
(1994). Edition: 26.

98. THE PARSIFAL MEDAL
by Gerald Laing, 1993.
Cast bronze. 125mm. Cast by the Royal
Mint. *The Medal*, no. 24 (1994). Edition: 25.

99. GWYNIAD
by Bethan Williams, 1993.
Cast silver. 90 x 80mm. Cast by Ginacliff.
The Medal, no. 24 (1994). Edition: 23.

100. GWYNIAD
by Bethan Williams, 1993.
Cast silvered pewter-based metal. 90 x
80mm. Cast by Ginacliff. *The Medal*, no. 24
(1994). Edition: 89.

101. YIN-YANG
by Dora de Pedery-Hunt, 1994.
Cast bronze. 87mm. Cast by Lunt.
The Medal, no. 25 (1994). Edition: 23.

102. IN MEMORY OF JOSEPH CONRAD
by Ewa Olszewska-Borys, 1994.
Cast bronze. 100 x 100mm. Cast by the
artist. *The Medal*, no. 25 (1994). Edition: 66.

103. SAX
by Karen Emerton, 1994.
Cast bronze. 87 x 54mm. Cast by the Royal
Mint. *The Medal*, no. 25 (1994). Edition: 10.

104. ALAS
by Deborah Sadler, 1994.
Cast bronze. 112 x 84m. Cast by Bronze
Age. *The Medal*, no. 25 (1994). Edition: 10.

105. ERIC GILL
by John Skelton, 1994.
Cast bronze. 130mm. Cast by Lunt.
The Medal, no. 25 (1994). Edition: 57.

106. THE VELLINGER MEDAL
by Tom Phillips, 1994.
Cast bronze. 97mm. Cast by Lunt.
The Medal, no. 26 (1995). Edition: 61.

107. PAVEMENT SERIES MEDAL NO. 1
by Robin Shelton, 1995.
Cast bronze. 72 x 72mm. Cast by Lunt.
The Medal, no. 26 (1995). Edition: 29.

108. TOMB ROBBERS
by Guy Richardson, 1994.
Cast bronze. 108mm. Cast by E.J. Blackley
& Son. *The Medal*, no. 27 (1995).
Edition: 45.

109. BENJAMIN BRITTEN
by Marika Somogyi, 1995.
Cast bronze. 78 x 63mm. Cast in the United States. *The Medal*, no. 27 (1995). Edition: 30.

110. BUDE WAVES
by Ron Dutton, 1995.
Cast bronze. 94 x 98mm. Cast by Lunt. *The Medal*, no. 28 (1996). Edition: 28.

111. CHERNOBYL
by Oxsana Teryokhina and Natalya Domovitskikh, 1995.
Cast bronze. 120mm. Cast in Ukraine. *The Medal*, no. 28 (1996). Edition: 40.

112. BLESSED ARE THOSE WHO HUNGER AND THIRST FOR JUSTICE'S SAKE FOR THEY SHALL BE SATISFIED
by Denise de Cordova, 1995.
Cast bronze. 58 x 69 x 30mm. *The Medal*, no. 29 (1996). Edition: 5.

113. BLESSED ARE THOSE WHO ARE PERSECUTED FOR JUSTICE'S SAKE FOR THEIRS IS THE KINGDOM OF HEAVEN
by Denise de Cordova, 1995.
Cast bronze. 65 x 65 x 36mm. *The Medal*, no. 29 (1996). Edition: 4.

114. BLESSED ARE THOSE WHO MOURN FOR THEY SHALL BE COMFORTED
by Katharine MacCarthy, 1995.
Cast bronze. 76 x 62 x 58mm. *The Medal*, no. 29 (1996). Edition: 5.

115. BLESSED ARE THE POOR IN HEART FOR THEY SHALL SEE GOD
by Katharine MacCarthy, 1995.
Cast bronze. 43 x 72 x 68mm. *The Medal*, no. 29 (1996). Edition: 2.

116. BLESSED ARE THE POOR IN SPIRIT FOR THEIRS IS THE KINGDOM OF HEAVEN
by Brian McCann, 1995.
Cast bronze. 60 x 65 x 15mm. *The Medal*, no. 29 (1996). Edition: 4.

117. BLESSED ARE THE MERCIFUL FOR THEY SHALL OBTAIN MERCY
by Brian McCann, 1995.
Cast bronze. 74 x 66 x 8mm. *The Medal*, no. 29 (1996). Edition: 2.

118. BLESSED ARE THE MEEK FOR THEY SHALL INHERIT THE EARTH
by Anne-Marie Watkins, 1995.
Cast bronze. 50 x 50 x 50mm. *The Medal*, no. 29 (1996). Edition: 3.

119. BLESSED ARE THE PEACEMAKERS FOR THEY SHALL BE CALLED THE SONS OF GOD
by Anne-Marie Watkins, 1995.
Cast bronze. 94 x 41 x 41mm. *The Medal*, no. 29 (1996). Edition: 4.

120. WILLIAM MORRIS
by Cecilia Yau, 1995.
Cast bronze. 205 x 65mm. (opened). *The Medal*, no. 29 (1996). Edition: 62.

121. MICHAEL AYRTON
by Ian Rank-Broadley, 1996.
Cast bronze. 100 x 100mm. Cast by the Royal Mint. *The Medal*, no. 29 (1996). Edition: 59.

122. AND THEN SHE MADE THE LASSES, O
by Hazel White, 1996.
Cast bronze. 87 x 72mm. Cast by Jack Spencer (Goldsmiths) Ltd. *The Medal*, no. 29 (1996). Edition: 52.

123. KONRAD LORENZ
by Veronika Fűz, 1996.
Cast bronze. 94mm. Cast in Hungary. *The Medal*, no. 30 (1997). Edition: 30.

124. WALKING
by Dana Krinsky, 1996.
Cast bronze. 102mm. Cast in Israel. *The Medal*, no. 30 (1997). Edition: 42.

125. HUMANITY MEDAL
by Dhruva Mistry, 1994/7.
Cast bronze. 95mm. Cast by the Royal Mint. Patinated by Arch Bronze. *The Medal*, no. 31 (1997). Edition: 49.

126. A HUMAN MIND IS UNFATHOMABLE
by Bernd Göbel, 1996.
Cast bronze. 97 x 94mm. Cast by Lunts Casting. *The Medal*, no. 31 (1997). Edition: 17.

127. RHYTHMS AND CIRCUITS
by Bill Scott, 1997.
Cast bronze. 112mm. Cast by Lunts Casting. *The Medal*, no. 31 (1997). Edition: 7.

128. OUR WORLD
by Bill Woodrow, 1997.
Cast bronze. 50 x 35mm. Cast by Niagara Falls Castings. *The Medal*, no. 31 (1997). Edition: 65.

129. JOIE DE VIVRE
by John Lobban, 1995/6.
Cast bronze. 90mm. Completed by Avril Vaughan. Cast by the Royal Mint. *The Medal*, no. 31 (1997). Edition: 36.

130. JOIE DE VIVRE
by John Lobban, 1995/6.
Cast silver. 90mm. Completed by Avril Vaughan. Cast by the Royal Mint. *The Medal*, no. 32 (1998). Edition: 12.

131. IN GOOD HANDS
by Roger McGough, 1997.
Cast bronze. 92 x 75mm. Modelled by Ron Dutton. Cast by Lunts Castings. *The Medal*, no. 32 (1998). Edition: 35.

132. THE GARDEN OF EDEN
by Gustaaf Hellegers, 1997.
Cast bronze. 95mm. Cast in The Netherlands. *The Medal*, no. 32 (1998). Edition: 47.

133. AFOREMENTIONED AFTERTHOUGHT
by Sara Ewers, 1997.
Cast bronze. 78mm. Cast by Lunts Castings. *The Medal*, no. 32 (1998). Edition: 14.

134. MONDAY MORNING
by John Paddison, 1997.
Cast bronze. 135 x 152mm. Cast by Lunts Castings. *The Medal*, no. 32 (1998). Edition: 29.

135. THE DREAMER
by Stanislaw Cukier, 1996.
Cast bronze. 110 x 106mm. Cast in Poland. *The Medal*, no. 33 (1998). Edition: 25.

136. ISOLATE
by Jane Sedgwick, 1998.
Cast bronze. 44 x 78 x 24mm. Cast by Heanes & Son. *The Medal*, no. 33 (1998). Edition: 48.

137. UNDISTURBED NIGHT
by Irene Gunston, 1998.
Cast bronze. 90mm. Cast by the artist. *The Medal*, no. 34 (1999). Edition: 22.

138. PERSPECTIVE ILLUSIONS: CUBE III
by Kate Harrison, 1998
Cast bronze. 65 x 61mm. Cast by the artist. *The Medal*, no. 34 (1999). Edition: 16.

139. LOVES' WATCH
by Felicity Powell, 1998
Cast bronze. 67mm. Cast by Aron McCartney. *The Medal*, no. 34 (1999). Edition: 12.

140. DAY DREAMING
by Tony Spinks, 1998
Cast bronze. 87 x 120mm. Cast by Lunts Casting. *The Medal*, no. 34 (1999). Edition: 10.

141. LEDA AND THE HAT-PIN
by Linda Crook, 1999.
Cast bronze. 78mm. Cast by Bronze Age. *The Medal*, no. 35 (1999). Edition: 31.

142. CHAMELEON
by Theresa Radcliffe, 1999.
Cast bronze. 82 x 90mm. Cast by Lunts Casting. *The Medal*, no. 35 (1999). Edition: 30.

143. NATURE AND TIME
by Geoffrey Clarke, 1999.
Cast bronze. 77mm. Cast by Nautilus Fine
Art Foundry. *The Medal,* no. 35 (1999).
Edition: 42.

144. GUIDED BY UNKNOWN INSTINCTS
by Judy McCaig, 1999.
Cast bronze and gold leaf. 63 x 86mm. Cast
by Pesarrodona, Barcelona. *The Medal,* no.
35 (1999). Edition: 20.

145. GAMUT IN AN ARMOIRE
by Alison Branagan, 1999.
Cast bronze and silver. 66 x 44 x 28mm.
Cast by BAC Castings. Assembled by the
artist. *The Medal,* no. 35 (1999). Edition: 15.

146. GAMUT IN AN ARMOIRE
by Alison Branagan, 1999.
Cast bronze. 66 x 44 x 28mm. Cast by BAC
Castings. Assembled by the artist.
The Medal, no. 35 (1999). Edition: 8.

147. MILLENNIUM MEDAL
by Felicity Powell, 1999.
Struck silver. 63mm. Struck by the Royal
Mint. *The Medal,* no. 36 (2000). Edition: 65.

148. ROUND IN CIRCLES - MILLENNIUM
MEDAL
by Paul Ryan, 1999.
Cast bronze. 90mm. Cast by Niagara Falls
Castings. *The Medal,* no. 36 (2000).
Edition: 35.

149. ZEBRA
by Robert Cook, 1999.
Cast bronze. 104 x 95mm. Cast by Lunts
Casting. *The Medal,* no. 36 (2000).
Edition: 47.

150. NIGHT SCAPE
by Roger Hannam, 1999.
Cast bronze. 70 x 65mm. Cast by the artist.
The Medal, no. 36 (2000). Edition: 24.

151. THE AIMS OF LIFE ARE THE BEST
DEFENCE AGAINST DEATH
by Paul Coldwell, 2000.
Cast bronze. 102mm. Cast by the Crucible
Foundry. *The Medal,* no. 37 (2000).
Edition: 11.

152. ROMANI JIVAPEN JINAPEN
by Daniel Baker, 2000.
Cast bronze. 98mm. Cast by the Crucible
Foundry. *The Medal,* no. 37 (2000).
Edition: 28.

153. SLEEPING TABLET
by Carole Dodds, 2000.
Cast bronze. 75 x 55mm. Cast by Falmouth
College of Arts. *The Medal,* no. 38 (2001).

154. ELLE
by Yvette Gastauer-Claire, 2000.
Cast bronze. 110 x 107mm. Cast by Butzon
& Berker GmbH. *The Medal,* no. 38 (2001).

155. SQUAMA
by Tim Cunliffe, 2001.
Cast bronze. 57 x 104mm. Cast by Lunts
Casting. *The Medal,* no. 39 (2001).

156. PAST AND PRESENT
by Rob Wood, 2001.
Bronze, steel and magnets. 78mm.
(diameter). Manufactured by the artist.
The Medal, no. 39 (2001).

157. PERPETUAL MECHANIC COMPOSITION I
by Bálint Bolygó, 2001.
Cast bronze. 110 x 100mm. Cast by
Edinburgh College of Art. *The Medal,*
no. 39 (2001).

158. DREAMS OF A DYING MOTH
by Lucy Willow, 2000.
Cast bronze. 70 x 65mm. Cast by Falmouth
College of Arts. *The Medal,* no. 40 (2002).

159. LINLITHGOW THRESHOLD
by Simon Beeson.
Cast bronze. 79 x 79 x 21mm. Cast by
Niagara Falls. *The Medal,* no. 40 (2002).

160. THE WORLD'S MY OYSTER
by Elisabeth Koster, 2001.
Cast bronze. 86 x 59mm. Cast by Lunts
Casting. *The Medal,* no. 40 (2002).

161. INHUMAN BEING
by Edoardo Lucci, 2001.
Cast bronze. 85mm. Cast by Lunts Casting.
The Medal, no. 40 (2002).

NOTE
The edition numbers for the earlier medals,
though broadly accurate, may sometimes
overestimate and more rarely underestimate
(e.g. 15, 45) the number actually made.

INDEX OF BAMS ARTISTS